The Many Deaths of

Inocencio Rodriguez

The Many Deaths of
Inocencio Rodriguez

· poems ·

ILIANA ROCHA

TUPELO PRESS

North Adams, Massachusetts

The Many Deaths of Inocencio Rodriguez
Copyright © 2022 Iliana Rocha. All rights reserved.

ISBN-13: 978-1-946482-64-8
Library of Congress Cataloging-in-Publication Data
Identifiers: LCCN 2021029499 | ISBN 9781946482648 (paperback)
Subjects: LCSH: Murder--Poetry. | Death--Poetry.
Classification: LCC PS3618.O3389 M36 2022 | DDC 811/.6--dc23
LC record available at https://lccn.loc.gov/2021029499

Cover and text design by Ann Aspell.
Cover art: Detail from "The Burial" by José Guadalupe Posada (1852-1913) Courtesy of the Art Institute of Chicago

This project is supported in part by an award from the National Endowment for the Arts

First paperback edition February 2022.

Tupelo Press
P.O. Box 1767
North Adams, Massachusetts 01247
(413) 664-9611 / Fax: (413) 664-9711
editor@tupelopress.org / www.tupelopress.org

Tupelo Press is an award-winning independent literary press that publishes fine fiction, non-fiction, and poetry in books that are a joy to hold as well as read. Tupelo Press is a registered 501(c)(3) non-profit organization, and we rely on public support to carry out our mission of publishing extraordinary work that may be outside the realm of the large commercial publishers. Financial donations are welcome and are tax deductible.

for my grandparents,

Inocencio (1922-1971) & Isabel Rodriguez

Table of Contents

Hoax

True Crime Addict

I know this from all the stories;
I do not have a body for it.

—MOLLY McCULLY BROWN

I want to be able to hold
the why in my hands

—ROXANE GAY

The Many Deaths of Inocencio Rodriguez

In this version, he was mistaken for Walt Disney

because he ventriloquized all the animals running loose in the neighborhood, those underfed, those collarless—

> spoke through their bodies because he couldn't synchronize his sound of defeated trumpets & gasoline

tanks, empty hitting the cement, with the family's demo reel.

The woman he left them for was in full, three-strip Technicolor like the kind you'd find in Houston's best-worst titty bars, performing a

> personal dance (table, friction, etc.) while oil tycoons were healed out of their wheelchairs. Think less Anna Nicole Smith, less 7-Up Factory, less DS, more Raincoater.

An alligator dancing with a hippo. No Christmas tree of money around her thigh, just a brief sketch of an in between pose to perfect the transition from

> pucker to kiss. *Fantasia*'s demons boast the breasts of a wooden masthead, the nipples of a chihuahua, skin the

color of Inocencio's lungs in perpetual state of collapse, failed by radioisotope cobalt & gamma rays.

> Ghosts whisked out of their shoeboxes, Detroit's mob pitchforked, they mistook his Spanish for unintelligible Texas slang that tumbled from underneath his moustache like translucent imps.

Español?! More like *a spaniel!*

A police officer said with his gun: *Off with his head.*

OFFICE OF THE MEDICAL EXAMINER
Wayne County, Michigan
John F. Burton, M.D.
Medical Examiner
400 E. Lafayette Avenue
Detroit, Michigan 48226

FILE NO. _____
AUTOPSY NO. _____

BAD HOMBRE

The Jump

He said that the millisecond after he jumped off the Golden Gate Bridge, he regretted it. After a long year, he felt tethered to the Bay Area's horizon, his future in beads & skimming the surface like fog. Mid-air, his bones split & feathered—he was lightness. His bones were braided wheat. Bones collapsed like a birdhouse of Popsicle sticks. He said his hands transmuted into doves, in a constant state of ascent like an apology. Apology, adjacent to the guilt that didn't belong to anyone—not his father, not himself, not that damaged womb he managed to successfully depart. *Is Kevin alive?* the refrain he knew would always belong to him, just as a phone's trill is to his father: his mother's birth control unused like a patient rotary dial. There was a suicide note pinned to his collar, & it simply read *Burden*. "10-31" is the code for bridge jumpers, & only nineteen other people have called luck by its name. When Kevin was rescued, he shivered like new sperm, & the Coast Guard wrapped him in a felt blanket, precursor to something like Kendrick Johnson's body. They were both missing a shoe. No one knows why one survived & why one died. *What does it mean to be living proof?*

The Many Deaths of Inocencio Rodriguez

Chain reaction of sugar dust explosions. Sugar cane, very, very blade.

The Many Deaths of Inocencio Rodriguez

A fistfight of paper on the ground, his *hello*
as ancient as dinosaurs. Honeydews
bright as crayons.
                    His donations to the sun,
the backbreaking work of immigrants. Human
battery. Decades of floral on the walls.

Lavender & homicidal, dusk. Everyone
in witness protection like Isabel's recklessness.
                    Where her spirit relocates,
she carries a fruit knife in her garter. Smokes grass
in the Badlands. But here, with a dandelion's

hostility, she robs dough from its shape
while he webs fetish into himself under running
water cold. Her apron
                    weighed down by niños
& migraine. The mescal tastes of nectar &
heatstroke, the curdled milk, a hazy observer.

Time measured by eyetooth's length, their bodies
nomads to each other, they fill jars
with night in order
                    to fool chronology, but night
can't fool anything except for moths, profanity—
& these godless American orphans.

Tabloid for Inocencio Rodriguez

Babcock said Rodriguez turned & fired on him
with a carbine. Breaking up a gunfight,
he said. Patrolman David Babcock, more phantom

than this man we've put back together, limb
for [   ]. Wound for [   ], bloodlights.
Babcock said, Rodriguez turned & fired on him,

so he aimed right for the guilt, American schism
between a Chicano's grace & [   ].
We said, Patrolman David Babcock, more phantom

in history's catalogue of [   ]. We ransom
the dead, American birthmark. American alibi?
Babcock said, Rodriguez turned & fired on him

until Inocencio was xerographic & hologram,
our universally-accepted truth, incoherent light.
[   ] said [   ] cock [   ] phantom.

As Inocencio Rodriguez evolves past superstition,
we're each an apology of *haunt*, for *goodbye*:
[   ] [we] turn & fire on hi[s]
[   ] phantom.

Bird Atlas

When Our Lady of Guadalupe arrived, she was heartbroken. At her feet, a pigeon crushed under the weight of a Ford 4x4, preserved in its own feathers & blood. She couldn't discern a skull, just a small boundary between where death was stamped onto concrete & where it wasn't.

After 600 years, this wasn't the first thing she wanted to see. Of course, she expected loss, but not its bones like Galveston seashells—you can barely find a lightning whelk or moon snail in one piece on those shores. Texas carelessness.

In the chapel built for her, there was cookware with intricate paintings on them. Juan Diego worked eight hours decorating a stone plate with roses, before there was a word for *art*. Another plate was adorned with Cuitlacoche comun's delicacy, gray & arched like a wave. Her tilma wasn't art. It wasn't a sign or even a map. It was the future in bright red echoes.

Humanity, Guadalupe thought, was more like the stubborn laughing chihuahuas, not like Mexico City canaries & their stupid wistfulness. She crouched closer to the ground to examine the bird atlas, wept in tangled ribbons & tributaries.

The Many Deaths of Inocencio Rodriguez

~~An avocado walks into a bar & orders a drink.~~

~~A father walks into a bar with a horse.~~

~~A fog walks into a bar.~~

A man walks into a bar & orders a glass of fluid daisies.

      A woman walks into a bar & undresses her lips on his glass' rim, half-mirrored. Stain of Upper Peninsula he cleans away with his thumb, turns into a streak of pink light no one's ever been able to capture in paint. *To capture* should not mean *to reflect*. He carries his grief alongside him, a colostomy bag filled with gray urine. She gets this or doesn't get this. It doesn't matter.

A man walks into a bar & vows to raise hell to honor drunk men & lonely women everywhere. Their blues exorcised from the dusty acoustic he plucks at. Minor chord, broken arm, cracked neck, glass undoing its liquid, undoing its stuck, minor chord, minor chord, major, liver, shot glass, shot glass, shot glass, darting crystal wood thrush. A jawbone soaked in mop water like a zygote. A couple making up the rumba as they go along, boleros, canciones, Rosa Carmina. *Sí, es ella.*

Landscape with Graceland Crumbling in My Hands

A man hits on a woman, as Elvis would,
as subtle as a pool cue to the chest,
as careless as gunplay, a chandelier victim, as all
things covered in crystal are, like the studded rhinestone
suits displayed in a manner fit for mourning.
There is no celebration, despite the lights'
unconvincing attempts at glamour, each vitrine,
a confessional booth covered in lipstick graffiti,
the lumen brightness alternating in waves of what feels
like Catholic guilt & drunkenness, 1,000 years of Saturday nights
crammed into the baritone prayer of bass guitar crumbling from a speaker.
Another woman weeps at the surprise of his gravesite, there,
situated by the stillborn twin's, a cloud Elvis tried unsuccessfully to move
all his life. The horses, too, know better, as their black shields
paint their view very, very forward.

The Many Deaths of Inocencio Rodriguez

Crooked on the wall, paintings of desperate
seagulls crude in their acrylic.
Little clouds of butter
bubble in her saucepan. Tonight,

a spider scares her into bed
instead of her fidelity—mythological as Pegasus,
he said. But hers is as common
as a bicuspid raw & twitching without
its wings.
All the fireworks

outside leave a gun the same way
his letters escape from a drawer. *Where is the dollar
in the morning?* Maybe under a pillow,
maybe the dead sparrow.

An inverted volcano, the uterus,
erupts its troubled
namesake better than the way he's destroyed
cities, she says. She hates
how he loved the world as if it were
a photograph.

Bury Them

I type my ex-boyfriend's name, press *Enter*. Amongst the few photos of him, I come across one of a serial killer, a woman—they happen to share the same name. All I can think, *This van is covered in dust like when it rains in Arizona.* A white woman, blond. Killed & raped her sister, Tammy, & two other teenage girls—her eyes out of the window are blank butter knives.

> He wore cacti like a novice & wore love like cacti, & like love, he left early.

> He missed California so much, he drew the state on notebook paper. Then, he built a plane to fly there, & I assembled, held the wind steady.

The killer was released from prison & now volunteers at a school, despite feeding Tammy animal tranquilizers until she choked to death on a monsoon of retch.

> The only photos he took of the desert were Hole-in-the-Rock, with its yawns in sandstone, & one flickering streetlight, a dreamless torch going cadaver.

Love Letter to Scott Peterson

Scott Peterson, the man who was convicted of murdering his wife and unborn child, had been on Death Row barely an hour when the first proposal arrived from a woman who wants to be the new Mrs. Scott Peterson.

—2005 NEWS ARTICLE

What was Paris like on New Year's? I have a tin figurine of the Eiffel Tower, about two inches tall, & it's the sorta thing I always want to keep in my pocket, along with a JFK photo in swan origami. Oh, & the fireworks! I bet the fireworks were something else. Like this vicious streak I have in me, were they like that? Diagrams hot with pride? The moment after they pop, that irreverent hiss, the kind hugging together two radio stations, a whippit in exclamation point. I love how a river tries to wind the colors together, but the sky is all gray skeleton, my body inside out & Velcro. Once I was told to chase my fear, but my fear is so close to my obsession, I can't tell the difference, & that's what led me to you, Scott. Do you believe in random acts of kindness? Gosh, you look so much like a brother I've always failed at rescuing. I'm afraid of growing old without someone there to take care of me, but I'm more terrified of being a mother. I get why you'd do it, if you did. Motherhood is just sucking desperately at an oxygen tank's exposed, detachable breast. Would you ever consider getting married again? Wouldn't it be funny for our wedding cake to be a chocolate bar, the vending machine our priest? I too am hated by the world—I'm a cat on fire in a metal drum. No one's looking for who put me there.

I Watched a Bat Kill Itself in Yuma

because of the heat. It flew into a metal sign, & we splashed it with water to cool it down, revive it. The water hit the concrete in a sizzle like a sigh while another 1999 girl stays unidentified, although her new name is something like *Homicide*. Yuma County Jane Doe. State of Remains: Not recognizable—traumatic injuries. I see she lassoed the moon & stars around her neck, & now it makes sense why Arizona has had record-breaking heat. The planes can't even fly. No one makes the connection between the way she preserves the galaxy & heat's lack of mercy. Like Mars, her face freckled with blood. Once the bat's eyes opened, we gave it some water to drink, but then it drowned itself. She keeps the darkness, & we stretch the universe like polymer. If we press putty to a newspaper, will it pick up the print? All this time, we've been afraid of the headline, but not the impenetrable smudge that's left.

Last Seen

answering an ad on Craigslist ISO BBW

going on a blind date with his air mattress mistress

filing my nails into coffins for pillbugs

Sylvia June Galvan last seen in Mt. Morris, Michigan.

sewing Pangaea's patchwork together as if it were initials into my panties

scraping the serial numbers off my breast implants

twisting into a carousel's golden rod to stab porcelain & sorbet

with death's compass rose of vultures

Jessica Heeringa last seen at her job at a gas station in Norton Shores, Michigan.

Jessica Suarez last seen jogging on the lakefront of Lake Michigan.

threading a needle through a tornado to keep it put like my father

exploding a bird with my fastball

doing my makeup: rouge noir, dolce, instant light peached, Lana

while Aunt Elma dyes my hair purple

chewing the inside of a Natural Bridge Cavern's cheek, whittling stalagmites

as a fountain of blood in the shape of a girl

Shawne Mellios last seen leaving her northern Michigan Home.

slamming the front door of my house on Taylorcrest

twerking

using a deer's corpse as a pincushion

while my father chants *like this & like this & like this & like this*

building Wrigley Field out of my ribs

being called *bitch*

Paige Renkowski last seen on westbound Interstate 96.

giving birth to my mother

posing as grace, a pine tree's latitude

crawling into the echo of Pearl Thompson's guitar riffs

stuffing myself into a duffel bag & putting it into the trunk

not taking myself seriously

pulverizing Lake Michigan into the size of a bladder

Chelsea Bruck last seen at a Halloween party dressed as Poison Ivy.

flirting with a zipper's split tongue as it divides into Gemini's boredom

tattooing the Imperial Sugar logo on the off ramp of my thigh

giving my best to all my exes

peering through the curtain of legs into my father's bedroom

tripping over my Spanish's uneven sidewalks

being buried without a straw in the forests off 131

pregnant with a deer's corpse

following the stuttering cirrus clouds into a decapitated arrow

Elegy for a Quinceañera Dress

Layers of tulle are just another method of *careful*. Dos Equis wounded all down the front, a handsy uncle, the taste of anger behind his teeth all salt, lime, & pilsner. They forgave him again because that's what the mariachi's trumpets command, *levántate de mañana, mira que ya amaneció*. The dress spun until it tangled like a telephone cord, until it was inside another dress, until its prediction was flamethrower, as she spilled out of it like fire's closest friend. Crystals hand sewn onto satin like the city skyline onto the night's velour, done by three women in Mexico. For each jewel, they recited a prayer, the same one as her grandmother as she smoothed a raw egg over her temples after he touched her. Those migraines, the owl pellets she dissected in biology, filled with hair & bones. Dress, a curtain closing. Crumpled panties, a doorknob to the future, her tía used to remind her. A slow dance with her father, the acrobatic & bionic minute hand. Paw prints in red clay around the hem when the hour finally hatched.

Milieu

If a tree falls in a forest, we hear it because it's you. The sound it makes is *hijo,
hijo, hijo*, as it isn't a forest, but a six-story window. If we tell you we're afraid,
you'll end up even more than dead, a rapid explosion of boyness. If I admit,
I don't think you have a heart, just a broken lamp beneath your chest, you'll
fracture another space, & that's the darkness where we'll be forced to live. If
I say, I worry you'll leave the dog strangled, you'll pull another window from
a room so that I can't see its burial. Why we hate so deeply our own: brother,
Mexican, brother, Mexican. Who do you think builds our houses? We need
a new word for *forest*, something that captures the height of looking beyond
woe. *Genitalia* has a certain ring to it, a wind chime, soft sound wrinkling
like bark. For describing mockery of the body, maybe *jigsaw*. There's no way
to soothe the carnivore of you, but your steps on the ledge come close, a brief
hush stamped in rubber. A sucker punch of stillness before the great leap:
Good morning, world!

Landscape with Boy-on-Boy Action

like
an interrupted orgasm gardenias torn
from the bush
crushed against pavement   you come
out again—

he, on top,
as   perfect as denim
your ass, an ampersand

he screams out each silence
in your history   but
nothing
is ever really joined   except

your cries double
                        &&
never a good son or athlete or man I'm
sorry
I've failed you

Like a girl, he was always
trading in what little
                        he owned of his life.
Already
he was too fragile for the world.

so many versions of Texas, Big
Bends: scorpions clustered…

a fist
            is thinking about every misery,
how each takes the shape of our
bodies

like a ruined building   a hip-hop
star   in a bubble bath up to her tits
her hair
exclaims in pink

all our televisions blurred in
the background   where we learned
sex's fictitious how-tos   he

isn't delicate to you   laughter &
blender
the ought-ought   leveling
itself on your shoulders

& the music continues, as gaudy as
a quinceañera   outspoken
mimicking the dangers   of

tradition

Tabloid for Judy Garland

[   ] we star in opposite directions,
                 a woman of her own grotesque—
    we've learned to be good at strangeness.

Her rainbow folded in half, she pled for a tenderness
                she was never given, confessed
[she's] learned to be good at strangeness,

the place where great joy meets even greater sadness.
               Voice of limping menthol bell, the best
    [   ] star [   ] opposite [   ],

her liver singing *ruin, ruin.* [   ] Reflection,
          a half-dead mirage of [   ]
    [   ] strangeness.

In red, she was skeletal & amphetamine, corrections
                for the mother, always one second
[away from reward]. We star in opposite directions,

[   ] but where has the protection
            been? *Home* is not a lesson:
               [   ] we star in opposite directions,
               we've learned to be good at strangeness.

White Mexican Girl

The rivers ran like couplets until they fell off the earth,
& she named each loss for its stone: *father, yesterday,*
chasing them across the water, until the muddy afterbirth

ruined what little clean was left of her socks. Mexico's mouth
open wide—like a row of blond dolls, maize stalks sang,
& the rivers ran like couplets until they fell off the earth,

her mother's geography at fault, dough covered in cloth
like a casket. A circle of vultures, like butts in an ashtray,
chase their reflections across the water, until the moon thirsts

itself dry like a widow. There, her first & last curse
strangling the trees, a rosary around her wrist, she obeyed
the rivers running like couplets, falling off the earth,

beer escaping a bottle's safety, diminutive amber urn
satisfied with each slow death. My mother's carefree slang
chastising snakes across the water, until it's adulthood's turn

to forget: *I love you, meeeeeeha, my little core-a-zone,* burning
        like history in reverse.

Self-Portrait as Crime Scene

What is happiness before it is blood on the wall & paint on the body? Who put what where? What is this stone-cold gibberish called *gunshot*, called *wound*? The room is evolving past poultry to dishwater. O, that habitual liquor, habitual five o'clock shadow parading as wisdom's cloud. If we were to autopsy divinity—where the lungs should be, another woman dead on the floor, called *accidental*. Called *suicidal*, & we'd bury her like another sponge.

These places slowly surrender the shapes of the women they've lost, but her spirit circles like a migraine—she ain't going nowhere except each mirror. Torture songs stab louder than the sound of history's *bang* from a revolver. Who misplaced the echoes? His desire, junkyard confidence, it strangles brightness from the rose. All I want is to grow arms & legs, to hogtie & bloodstain the beefcake.

Kurt Cobain Requiem (Acoustic)

Are you filming us?

—Courtney Love

A bullet to the brain, a Dodge spits & backfires—
I think I'm dumb or maybe just happy—in reverse
through the Seattle streets. Hands, as limp as his feet,
like two suffocated doves. We listened to his voice—

I think I'm dumb or maybe just happy, in reverse,
rewound, dulling our cassette tapes—as if it told us
suffocating doves were echoes torn in half. His voice,
tethered, the brown ribbon to its supply reel,

rewound, dulling our cassette tapes—as if it told us
to rearrange our pulses, put a vein back in its place,
tethered, the brown ribbon of blood to its supply reel,
the heart: *I know this love of mine will never die.*

To rearrange our pulses, put a vein back in its place,
chase that first high, parades of cinder & blackout
through the heart: *I know this love of mine will never die.*
Soundtrack composed of minor chords: Closer, but not

quite that first high, cinder & blackout parade of love,
a guitar split down the middle. He took himself—our
soundtrack composed of minor chords—but
is there such as thing as resting in peace? We don't know.

A guitar split down the middle, he took himself—our
best times, our worst. Kurt Cobain is everywhere.
There is no such as thing as resting in peace, we know.

Tequila, Cinnamon, Orange

My father, such a glamorous drunk,
carelessly exposing his green Bonneville
glitter to Highway 59's thighs when he'd disappear for days.
Picked up the phone, said in his long-voweled cadence, I love you,
daughter, when-o, bye. I couldn't get it any other way. So purposefully near
his crotch, his belt buckle: JR it demanded, inviting women into the purple or turquoise
of his late-'80s Levi's.
                              Like a secretary, he'd stiletto his boot
heels when he entered a room, inspect his cuticles after each morning coffee. He would
disappear again. Those nights, I never slept, but I managed something like
exhaustion picturing him in the backyard, leaning his machismo
against a fruit tree. He was never real but imperial,
always keeping the women up—like the white
towers of the sugar factory stinging
the night's blank solitude—
never surprised by all
his sufferings.

Chelsea Bruck Requiem

Ash Township, Michigan

Please tell me, where is it safe for us? because it's not anywhere near the spindly torture of your hands: multiple fractures of the nose, eye sockets, & jaw. Because it's not anywhere near the spindly torture of the stars, flat & stunned, like her two chipped teeth, happiness erupted. The story goes, we are the apple of your chaotic hybrid, painting our skulls with dust & blush: multiple fractures of the nose, eye sockets, & jaw. Of the stars, those flat & stunned obelisks, stickerburs caught in our sweaters, we were always wrong—they never led us home, as the story goes. We are the chaos designed by rubbing two hipbones together, we were always wrong—they never led us home, those fossilized ears where you whisper sacred your danger. Designed by rubbing two hipbones together, a hollowness of absolutes, your loneliness: multiple fractures of the nose, eye sockets, & jaw. Those fossilized ears where you whisper sacred your danger like cologne, you put a gun there, a rock, your chiseled spank—a hollowness of absolutes, your loneliness. Your muscles shone metallic, the way you told the story.

IN THE PLACE OF GUESSWORK

OFFICE OF THE MEDICAL EXAMINER

Wayne County, Michigan
John F. Burton, M. D.
Medical Examiner
400 E. Lafayette Avenue
Detroit, Michigan 48226

FILE NO. ___8-71___
AUTOPSY NO. ___A71-9___
LAB. NO. _____

GROSS AUTOPSY FINDINGS

I, _____ _A.M._ _____, M.D., CERTIFY THAT I PERFORMED
THE AUTOPSY ON Incencio Rodriguez AKA John Doe #3 , DECEASED,
AND THAT THE ATTACHED DESCRIPTION IS CORRECT AND ACCURATE. IN MY OPINION THE CAUSE OF DEATH
IS _G.S.W. s — chest & abdomen._
_____
_____
_____

THE FOLLOWING DIAGNOSES CAN BE MADE ON THE BASIS OF THE ATTACHED DESCRIPTION:

1. G.S.W. I — left lower
    ant. chest.
    Penetration of the left
    lung and liver. TR–TR.

2. G.S.W. II — abdomen.
    Penetration of the left
    adrenal and kidney. TR–TR

3. G.S.W. — Rt. arm. TR–TR

I CONCUR IN THE ABOVE FINDINGS AND THE ATTACHED DESCRIPTION, HAVING PERSONALLY WITNESSED THE
DEMONSTRATION OF THE ABOVE FINDINGS:

4.

SIGNATURE: _Teizie Troozle M.D_

SIGNATURE: _____

8-19

Texas Seven

In a garage sharpening knives

> Joseph Christopher Garcia (born November 6, 1971,
> in San Antonio, Texas), on Texas Death Row awaiting execution.

Shiner Bock arranged on a card table,
a family of bottles: *I will fight you if you're just gonna
kill me.* A skull of amber glass,
malice, a napkin sticky to the bar where
a girl once left her name in lipstick: *Joslyn.*
Hammers cast their shadows of cheek & neck
on walls, a row of bibles
projecting their version of leather holiness,
a holster missing a gun. Always
a woman at the center of violence, her
blue cursive *A* a vein to his wrist
like a lasso humiliating
a bull's hind legs, nylon daisy-chained
around a hostage's prayer. Both trying to crawl
deep into the ground's safety
with the tick-tock of hoof & elbow.
I didn't stop stabbing until he stopped moving. There's no
such thing as safety—it's not ambulance,
it's not hearse, it's not the boar's
head frozen in a snarl, but that's close.
Rage: *I carry all of them with me.*

All was ocean

      Randy Ethan Halprin (born September 13, 1977, in McKinney, Texas), on Texas Death Row
      awaiting execution.

Babe, you know, when I was talking about nature, I was thinking about a place
where we could hear birds, or water, or a waterfall. Everything from sex

to a Sunday drive requires imagination, usurp, coup d'état, but I no
longer require privacy to arouse my wasted neodymium, twinned,

pointing in your direction of rose-colored salt I snort until I tarnish.
You know the story of my childhood better than I do because yours

is the lie I love: Tell me about how I used to fish with Papa, a black
bass hooked by the stalled question mark between father & son. I

saw his tenderness in the drop point against dorsal fin, scales gone
easily against the grain. Noncontact, other than a handshake

like a tulip unwound, every bit of intimacy I've created through
electrical signals & two ways, folie à deux, but I want you in grand

rond de jambe en l'air against the Congress Ave. Bridge, where bats
shatter the blank silhouette of silence like a mariachi band's brass

& ranchera tenor. No mitzvah for me, just acid trips & the sweltering
Pathéchrome dripping its *The Gulf Between*, where I fingered Grace

Darmond's shyness by way of her blistering pearls. A *yes* in each little
sun, a baby's skull of crushed seashells.

Hideout shuttered

Larry James Harper (September 10, 1963, in Danville, Illinois – January 22, 2001,
in Woodland Park, Colorado), committed suicide before he could be captured by law enforcement.

brother jim, brother
jim
brother slouched, brother
mantised
cathedral, garbage can a
sparkle away from being
blessed, from Mary's
viscera templated
in our Coachlight's
gold

Pillowcase, a drought ends

> Patrick Henry Murphy, Jr. (born October 3, 1961, in Dallas, Texas), on Texas Death
> Row awaiting execution.

No one   found me a country.   *Wander less*

means nothing when less is all   I give, the sky's
abstinence, stubborn-headed virgin—

I seethe at the offering of virga. Desire, Martian Cloud,

                I go left, heavy with music: *my, girl, my
girl*, sharp as a knife, silver aurora

rising thirsty to her throat. Brutality, the difference of
coulds, I picked one: *Hush, fey lucre,*

hush, high school crush.   Hearts in glitter pen, a sky-
line clustered with want,   a nightgown stripped

of its best silk XXX, lake-dark,

                I drowned lake-bottom.

Last words

Donald Keith Newbury (May 18, 1962, in Albuquerque, New Mexico – February 4, 2015, in Huntsville, Texas), *executed*.

each new indignity defeats only the body pampering the spirit with obscure merit

Going to die in another prism

Michael Anthony Rodriguez (October 29, 1962, in San Antonio, Texas – August 14, 2008, in Huntsville, Texas), *executed.*

the roses smell are grow in backyard yellow
masochism

i can't sheets of paper

this is between the mattress &

bed springs
& numerous photographs but became more than zoo

some other world for drones

& so & so

meticulous

it looks a little slip up nip slip

not that bound Corinthian

running a bomb per dollar

parody

dog collars

i grown a lil' problem   i'll

  my dues strains selling dishes

food we had de-boned had be   had beatable

    victims

     prepared as jewelry in the shop

rotated pop lock & shot $2,000

  cost me some other suffering

     maybe not copy scared me wow

prevented things are happening

   after

     & our moved to another

   larger prison

     just a bunch of earth involved & leaves us

Black to paint this vehicle with

George Angel Rivas, Jr. (May 6, 1970, in El Paso, Texas – February 29, 2012, in Huntsville, Texas), *executed*.

Before language was the afterlife & before
the afterlife, there was violence, the back
window we couldn't outrun. Blue & red
eclipses turned violet in their urgency, turned
cochlear implant, turned shot dead. We kept
saying we were lucky, they missed us by
three cars, but what did we ever know of
luck? Yes, we got past the Texas confluence,
where the Guadalupe meets the San Antonio,
twang meets drawl. We didn't impersonate
anyone we couldn't have been,
& that's what was terrifying. How many
lengths is 31 lives? We were not daring, we
were survivors. We took care of what little
was left of ourselves: Snatch & grab, my
friend. Break & enter, pal.

The Many Deaths of Inocencio Rodriguez

[   ] while in the smeared light of January, the steps icy, Isabel's *cuidado*: Don't be fooled by the man in the coffin. He is just a pale copy. [

this] pale copy, gurgled pity like he did blood. Spit his *lo siento* into a beer can. [   ] while in the smeared light of January, the icy steps, his brick-by-brick resurrection. The Ouija board mirror: A row of women in black, their hands [yellow roses holding tight the bloom]. A pale copy of the sun: love outstretched & growing arms, divinity a slow melt beneath our tongues. Inocencio limp, dragged [by his wrists   ], smear[ing the] light of January [   ] like her lipstick on his collar.

The dream was exactly like this [   ]:[   ] coffin.
[   ] .pale copy *father*, doing his due diligence to
[   ] violence, to power, to sex: [   ]
enshrined in blankness—In the smeared light of everything, his
[   ] body a pale copy thrumming [Bessie, Bessie, Bessie]

HOAX

Marfa Lights

There they are—our fears, animated. Highway 90's wide shoulder, into it, we cry. The scary thing about fear is that it hovers, remains stationary as it pulses on & off. A roadside sign here says *Crunch* instead of *Church*, despite the steeple's persistence, & like the sun, everything has slowed to a crawl in West Texas except in the way we name things: *will-o'-the-wisp, bad hombre, small fires*. In the way language fails at documenting our corruptions, the lights appear as a lesson in scattering. Who moved the backbone of Texas? Was it the Spanish, or was it the U.S.? Did Mexico have a say? Who carved *Fuck this* into the desk I used in junior high school history class? I'd love to meet them, ask them why their crude artwork looked so much like an abandoned asylum wall. Saltwater seeped into the bones of Galveston trees, killed 40,000 of them, & they're calling it an ecological disaster. I want to know what this feeling is in my bones, if it's saltwater killing me, or if it's something else, & if this something else has a name that lessens its intensity like *domestic violence*. How he moved my smile as if it were a Texas backbone. Ask me if I had a say in which rivers separated one state from another. The town where my mother was born, which had the largest sulfur deposits, now depleted & left *ghost*. The Lone Star has always gambled on disorientation, & it usually wins.

Ken Caminiti Dies in a Houston Hotel

off Highway 59, where it locks elbows with the 610 East
& West, Beltway 8, where the city converges in a concrete
knot, but all this time, they got it wrong—it wasn't this Houston,
it was the Bronx's speedball, & he wasn't fishnetted, gartered,
up to his nipples in silk, lipstick saddening his mouth more
than a country song could, call girls surrounding him like a
torn bouquet, ball gag ironically in Houston's 1996 MVP,
batting .326 with 40 home runs, 130 RBIs, & forearms
that could knock the shit out of an army of hecklers.
According to Houston, his body is buried in the Astrodome,
under the row of orange stadium seats, the exact row where my father
& I went to see the last game Caminiti ever played there, where I felt the seat
get wet with sex anticipation, those arms, that swing, that giant
bulge that seemed to symbolize third base, cheeks swollen with
chew like the bag where he'd rest his cleat. City officials are voting
on the Astrodome's future, but those seats are available to purchase
online, & I wonder if the 1962 Colt .45s' season is for sale, along with the place
where my father stood & wept for the racism in Texas, just after the first pitch, after
the picking cotton, El Campo, Moczygembas (a Polish nickname
for heavy drinker) that wouldn't sell him pastry, for inevitable infidelity
& alcoholism, how statistics quantifies things & he just can't,
Houston taking claim for a death, the nostalgic want behind that gesture,
like liquid liner & a throwback cut crease à la Nancy Sinatra, the myth
of exactitude in a line, time stopping at certain points on the body like full
bush pornography, the VHS hidden under my parents' bed, a woman named
Maria who stole my father, killed Caminiti, the hourglass shape in 8% of American
women, steroids, trying to undo a memory but how the enlarged heart
can't stand but to keep it close.

The Many Deaths of Inocencio Rodriguez

The headline read: "Man Seeks to Unravel Curse with Pants and Egg"

I needed a fresh glass of wife, so I went down to the local sorceress for help. She told me I needed an egg, a spoon, a nail, some pubic hairs & underpants. One hand cracked the egg below my waistband, & it wiggled down my cock—another word for *home*, the map that named America.

She charged me only $12,195 to take care of the curse, my mummified dinosaur. So magical, she kept a unicorn in a tablespoon, left shadows like loose change. I didn't anticipate her following me all over town, spying on me at the corner store in hiding with the pickles. When I walked outside, I saw she had keyed my car with phrases she hoped it would listen to: *smack, train here, xxxxxxxx.*

Learning how to tear apart the United States began slowly, as I put my cup of water on them. The glass began to sweat, first dissolving Dallas (Love Field) where a marriage dismantled easily. On to West Texas' mirror, a landscape of clay mountains & stars short-circuiting, an occasional firework that happened to be a plate breaking very close to the torn envelope of my face.

The Many Deaths of Inocencio Rodriguez

Her breasts, seagulls choking
      on cinnamon gum, hands as pale as dough.

Her center: neon catalpa, wet
      leaves that circle like West Texas vultures.

Her hair, an avalanche of grosgrain ribbon,
      divides the curtain from the window,

the window from its cartilage, cartilage
      from its piercing, the piercing from an ear,

an ear from gravity. His body incubates
      under the pile of XX bright with its blankness,

under a network of electric vines
      stubborn to a fence. The tugboat of his guilt

dragged home on a string from the river
      where he taught his son the impossible

bottle. *Ahogar*: to drown, wasps giving
      birth in the lungs. The menthol of Virginia Slims

forty-six years later. Black coral of blood
      gathered in the colon, in the throat, the liver.

      The antonym for *apology*.

Hoax

Sherri Papini was found alive on Thanksgiving Day, 2016. Sherri Papini was covered in purple & blue clouds she called bruises. Sherri Papini's long hair was cut because her abductors had an aversion to blondes. Sherri Papini insists they were two Latinas. Had that vague but familiar outline of otherness—accents nasal, sentences quick with vowels falling from a cliff: *ah, eh, ee, oh, oo*. One of the women had curly hair, thin eyebrows, & pierced ears. Sherri Papini described the other woman, who was older, as having thick eyebrows with straight salt-&-pepper hair. Sherri Papini is not Tera Smith who has been missing since 1998. Sherri Papini is not a supermom. Sherri Papini is exactly what my cousin Carrie wished she looked like, especially after my grandmother told her to stay out of the sun: *You prieta*. I want to say "Sherri Papini" over & over again until I reach semantic satiation, until I empty out all the marrow of meaning from her name. Sherri Papini insists her abductors did this with the word "flores"—one of the only words she remembered from high school. Her teacher made them all choose a name in Spanish. Hers was Margarita, for the daisy, not the drink. Now when she sees gumplant & poppy, she feels nothing, not even the scissors against her hair like a field of wheat.

The Many Deaths
of Inocencio Rodriguez

He took a swig of aquarium, swallowing the ovals
of pain covered in bronze scales. Isabel, led to
Texas by hopscotch & jump rope, eventually lost
her twins, in a warm broth of piss & motor oil, to
the braided nylon cords, holding the handles as if
they were her dying mother's hands in wood.
    We will inherit this sadness.
All the churches in General Bravo, Nuevo León
were lit on fire, cathedrals blurring the sky with
their easy praise. Mothers, buried in symmetry,
around an axis like a cloud stabbed with a
cigarette. Like a newborn on a flagpole, something
like praise at half-mast. Wounds he placed on her
body:
    Michigan's UP, state outline the spindles of
a deer's carcass on Highway 131, its legs a twilight
of pelt. The sternum when separating the hide,
the strange practice of a sigh. Blood, a headache
of tannins: *les pido perdón, tell me what is a holy
thing, can I combine these commas into skeletons?*
    Coccyx, suffix, spinal
tap, half an inch of tongue left in the backseat: his
intervals measured by plea & panadería. It was her,
pending—

Texts Killing Fields

At the spot where the girl lay, I see the refineries. Their stencils are blurred on the horizon, making their machinery less intricate, & therefore, holy. Her screams like steady streams of dark smoke. Simile fails at this. Her voice, like rubber, stretched only so far. I ask, what is fractionation? The whole is greater than, the field says. I ask, what is a cradle? Even the darkness has arms, the field replies. We are all filled with leaving, it continues. I cannot give them back because they were never mine. But whose were they, I want to know. We knew her by the dress, the field says, smelled sweet like almonds. We knew her by her overbite. Did she eat darkness, I ask. It crumbled between her molars like gravity. The field is gracious with its anonymity, stuck in the marsh with no way out but *no way out*. She dreamed that way too, I say, in infinity's lemniscate. She had it on her wrist & ankle, two unfortunate anchors. There's no delicacy in faith, the field says, just in the way the scavengers rearrange the bones.

The Many Deaths of Inocencio Rodriguez

The street hangs from the sky, held in suspension
by summer's dark hair lazily in a braid,
        exhausted power lines. Someone has thrown a pair
            of sneakers, joined together by knots,
over the wires, insistence of *we walk away from*.
    Or declaration of staying's ease. What's gathered
overhead—recognition of a cloud-shaped hurt.
              Happiness won't find a home here,
escapes through each home's latticework like papel
        picado chiseled down into a pair of doves.
    Hanging on the wall of my grandmother's kitchen,
a wooden scene of her kitchen, with its miniature pots & pans—
          on the tiny table, a vase of daffodils given
to her before he left. This scene never
    expands. It stays its little size, despite the trial &
        want for it to expand beyond is diminutive
yellow. Can we reposition La Llorona's creek behind
    another house? What must stay pinned to the map
like a butterfly: the view, the sugar factory where he worked
    when he at last modified Texas geography
to stretch all the way to Detroit
        by letting his gun follow his steps in the grass.

The Many Deaths of Inocencio Rodriguez

Duel: a half-step toward a flammable grin.

The Many Deaths of Inocencio Rodriguez

A full bladder—each dream this night—a continent in plasticity, a rubber water bottle trembling like a tendon's flexible twitch. Dying pecan trees with their kernels of air centers & fuzz, skeletons overcrowding the Texas grayness, fascinate me, as do Isabel's pinky toes

I've tried to solve with water gun & hose, but there is never an end to an affair. I undo the night's half-moon wedgie like a husk—corn, a row of fingers bitten down to their nubs. She tastes of the charred maize, mayonnaise, & lime that filled my cup. She tastes of the silver wrung from a spoon. At any given time, a crotch reeks of piss & someone shits their pants, a toilet bowl is filled with last month's blood. My daughter will always know my face as an elevator door closing, she will obsess over my cursive whose capital J's rise gimpy on the page, a prank of the self. Where the gun's muzzle has wounded, plant there a rose. It's as good as signing your own name.

PHX Elegy

Flowers' sad confidence, mostly carnation, petals boiled down into little globes, a homemade tree of a cross, smell of animals that also died here. The sidewalk stain rivals a pupil drained of its light. He hears my steps before I reach the door—*At the end of my suffering/there was a door*, a cluster in gray carnation, tin leaves & their accidental light. A crowd grieves into its hands, distorted globe pared down to its gores. Megacity stain. A burial of animal, leveled between infinity & knuckle, animals less the ancestor of us. His door shuts behind me as if I weren't. Stain of cyanotype, the sky slowly closes its carnation clouds, ammonium & piquant, globes cotton with mercy. Don't pour the light all over this. Light's recluse is friend to guilt's animal. Nitro-, neuro-, non-, empties of the globe, nitro-pistol, non-pistol, never-pistol trapdoor nitro-opens. He bauble, he carnation of honorary completion, he erotica, he of walk through colorful ash, he of walk-of-shame, he of night's half-interrupted light, disciple & nectar & carnation of dread in the crowd, in this bed, in the animals scratching on the easy pattern of a screen door because of night's urgent bladder, detrusor globe & fiber. His fingertips like a globe's curvature collapsed under chronology's weight, a walk of index & middle finger over my body, door to ink & hoax—light. Zipper me away, brass & denim animal, from grief taking on a carnation's wrinkles, bouquet underwired beneath my breasts, light doubled nude in globes. Animals devout in their indifference, flammable door of loss burst before us, carnations open wide in *no*.

The Many _____ of Inocencio Rodriguez

plural noun

Rosary

   Sleep's body resting like a Chevy 4x4 slammed into a tree. *Yeah, I lived,* it says, *as a million drunk ballerinas. As an arabesque upside down & backward. A papalote fractured. A windowsill made of broken tibias.*

   His ziggurat terraced by aggression, stone scored into steps like Isabel's hipbones. Nothing from him has ever escaped, not so much a microfiche wheeze or a lawnmower's razor-thin snore, not his carnival of women, buck tooth, ferris-wheeled, first kiss, & hiss. Light without radiance, a circle deviant under construction.

   Out of respect, birds drip the sky like stale coffee, dissimulate the parking lot where some automobiles stand unshelled. I shut my eyes the way I slam a door— puncture sleep, letting all this air out bored of its solitary room. His face is half-covered by blanket. He doesn't dream.

Mariachi/El Rey

   Night is a stairwell that sings its steps in metal & Spanish. *You let me go too easily,* the moon whispers to its shadow. A white rabbit jumping through a fence missing a picket, a sigh through his diastema—*I can't stay here anymore.*

   I can't.
   I can't.

The misery of history in short refrain. I think of hurting him—throwing a compass toward the vastness of West Texas' neon pink topography, my knuckles against his cheeks once adolescent with acne. The torrential rain of accordions: *Con dinero y sin dinero, yo hago siempre lo que quiero…*

Metaphor

The only thing decorating the chapel, a motorcycle. A motorcycle that never went anywhere.

The Many Deaths of Inocencio Rodriguez

When he traveled, he did so without mercy, in a body that was not a body but canvas painted with his handprints. It took 405 days to get to Detroit, & like each horse he passed, he stopped for a three-finger pour from an irrigation ditch. Wept for the solitary shoe missing its mate. Every morning was his last moment alive, & he was grateful for that kind of torture—say *asphyxia* until you run out of breath. We've all been underwater, our coats heavy with liquid & mirrors looking back at someone we've left. He was last seen down the street with the neighbor lady who remains protected now in her anonymity, a globe erased of its continents. All signs pointed north, far, far away from Mexico, the shape of whiskey spilled on a wooden table, gurgle, gurgle, & spit. Throw sawdust on vomit, the body is its own holy abattoir, carving away at its discoveries. Mystery, he always chased mystery, the sound of a triangle signaling dinner, damage done to the pig we were told not to love. Rod against steel, sound reminiscent of each ache we've had since he's been gone, inside us, an echo in search of its rattle.

Collective Memory

*From 1848 to 1928, mobs murdered thousands of
Mexicans, though surviving records allowed us to clearly
document only about 547 cases.*

—NEW YORK TIMES, FEB. 20, 2015

ten mexicans are dead, left to suffocate in a trailer, discovered
after the driver asked someone for a drink of water. the truck's
cooling system was broken, & that's one way to describe the
arrhythmia of our fumbling americana. bodies, their sorrows
boiling as if on a stove, vital organs melting plastic through
texas' fingers. we've left their dreams lifeless, dangling by the
necks, carotids wrung out to dry like old hand towels. my
grandmother pins clothes on a line—they give breeze back
for the wind to bear in a way skin can't. what violence gives
back to us is more of itself, & power gives us *delete, delete,
delete*. another mexican, interrupted from planting flowers
in a horse's skull, was bound to a mesquite & taught a lesson
about divinity's combustion. the lynch mob wasn't satisfied
until they couldn't tell his body from the bark. in san antonio,
authorities peel the bodies away from where they lie, but they
can't remove the wreckage from their faces: *deeper still is that
old trailer abandoned in victoria, the one with eighteen dead
mexican immigrants inside*...this is not plagiarism—this is
history in circles

The Many Deaths of Inocencio Rodriguez

Certain nights my father & I eclipsed
into & out of the shadow absences of the city
             streets, convinced home did not exist.

Our drive began with a song that hissed
& cracked through the honeycombs of speaker.
             Those nights my father & I eclipsed,

umbra with umbra. Spanish skewered onto an axis:
yo hago siempre lo que quiero, half-hearted debris
             of home. My juvenile & fugitive

hallucinations, driving through the neon's grit,
away from our mother & mistress deformities.
             Those nights we eclipsed,

lost & habitual. Metal & peripheral. In abyss,
gray & virtual. The Chevy's tires in full scream
             with a halt: *Home does not exist!*

             We were the chiseled antibodies
who left the sky matte, its blank confetti.
             Those nights my father & I eclipsed,
certain home did not.

Tabloid for the Black Dahlia

[   ] In the smeared light of everything, her body
like someone in a hurry to make [   ] a taffeta dress,
obliterated in a knife's dancing swarm, pale copy

[   ] after pale copy,
California's drought, the color of a watery Old Fashioned, nest
[of   ] the smeared light of everything, her body

finally understanding its longing, the honest artistry
of removing a smile from a face, [   ] happiness
obliterated in a knife's dancing swarm, pale copy,

a triplicate of flower tucked into a gumshoe's lapel, actuary
tallying risk & uncertainty, another man confesses
to [   ] smear[ing the] light of everything, her body

in trembling magazine font: *Here! is Dahlia's belongings*
Letter to follow, [   ] our obsession [   ] blessed
[by   ] a knife's dancing swarm, her body

bisected, doing its due diligence to [   ] violence,
to power, to sex: [   ] enshrined digitally—
          In the smeared light of everything, her [   ] body
          obliterated in a knife's dancing swarm, [Betty, Betty, Betty]

Still Life

for Aunt Carmen

Sorrow drizzles down, a gray feather, like a Vietnamese
woman painting the Virgin Mary's minutiae on an acrylic

nail, she taps her finger on the margarita glass, claims
the antihero for holiness is inside. What exactly have I evolved

past? *El Diablo no duerme* written in red lipstick on the edge
of her cup stuck with salt, & the clouds on hangers are like

my grandfather's blue satin Houston Oilers jacket, oil derrick
erect. Donkeys, globes, & assorted cartoon characters

half-cumbia from the ceiling by string, she takes out a CoverGirl
compact powder in the lightest shade, cakes on layers

in a way that no one understood when I did it in high school
in lieu of hanging out with the Mexican girls. The trumpets

& their relentless barking come by, serenading the table with "El
Rey," & she is never afraid to confront nostalgia: *Remember when we*

crumpled up the rice fields, put them tequila-lit in barrels? When Daddy
telegrammed himself back from Normandy? Our sticky mouths

of masa harina not a platitude, but a plea for domesticity
we disowned? As a little old woman behind glass pounds

dough into tortillas, we line our newborns up in neat rows,
build animals from shredded newspapers & papier-

mâché. I connect my skeleton with brass fasteners, adding a bow
to my mouth with too-dark lip liner.

The Many Deaths of Inocencio Rodriguez

Her body like the cactus needles of Arizona, as sharp as the clock's minute hand, blades of why, a mescal aftermath, Lake Michigan glass mistaken for shells & cherry, I like how she walks, how she dresses, her body an authority of lime & coconut, the jalapeño that punctures the tongue, part of the hand you lick before the self, the before & after of *amen*, tires & their rubber braids, a wince, her mother pulling her hair so tightly into a ponytail, all she remembers is the burn like being face first in snow, the unnamable sound of snow underneath a bike, an authority, crème de pistache & Mexican vanilla, cheeks swollen with mint & rum, the anti-collapse of ice, an authority of ass, chronic antidote, pucker up, the salt is her own spit, she wrings sex from the laundry, her body is slang, residue in a soap dish.

Elegy to the 1950s Waist

O, ye ghosts of an abandoned chandelier factory,
Buddy Holly's "Peggy Sue" exploding
shortly after take off similar to the joyous hollering
of Tequila! & dirty sax. *Bustier*,
how French of you, O, squeeze me tightly
until circumference disappears
into the yellow of tape measure. O, 38-18-36,
Betty Brosmer striped & behind
bars, her corset, year-round Christmas
lights strangling a wave, unlike
Botticelli's zaftig. Perpetual lap dance, even when
making tonight's meatloaf, a proto-
rap video vixen, but not vixen at all because
there was never any worry about who the sexiest
woman in the room was.

The Many Deaths of Inocencio Rodriguez

Hum/ hers, an indecisive rhythm, sometimes here, sometimes there, in between a cat's lungs, swimming the porch light's globe, the wandering shape of you when you died, afraid of silence, but why, little hum/

I remember your skeletal remains in an overrun garden/ her marble cake's delicate swirls that got more unruly with time, her gaze out the kitchen window, admiring the clouds' texture like a trashcan full of my/horse sketches done in pencil on cardstock. The trees gathered outside, their branches tangled but reaching toward some kind of logic/ a wire sculpture of a thoroughbred sitting on top of the China cabinet I will inherit from her, full of Mason jars, their lids inherently impossible when I'd crave homemade pepinillos that ruined the taste of others afterward like the first love/ I've never had

You taught me something about being/ blessed as glowing peaches canned in syrup/ my father making a mistake that wasn't really anything special, the disappointment of what it means to be la nieta, chillona. What more can be said about regret but/ regret—

that lithe rodent that seemed to outsmart all your poodles/

The Many Deaths of Inocencio Rodriguez

When the gold ran out, she crocheted
each star until her knuckles
collapsed, a piano exhausted
from the day's dirges [Lil Keke's "Chunk
Up the Deuce"], anthems for those
who unwillingly escaped Texas'
five-pointed blankness. *Star:*
another name for *smithereen,*
for *Detroit,* for the gun's firecracker
that shattered him, mirrors
draped in black cloth & rosaries
[Hail Mary, full of place].
She's always tried to outrun the dark erasing
her neon tornado of crushed Bakelite—
the memory of his body
unpacking its losses, lacquered
bloody, on a city street—
spiraling her into borealis.
[No me gusta la noche. Los avións, barcos.]
Reverse Guadalupe, silver-strained
by cigarette, if she could give back her daughters
to the womb, she would, follow
her disappearing
curls of smoke instead, resist
repair of her plastic organs.
Her wedding
[*ay, ay, ay, ay, canta y no llores*]
dress' papel picado lace,
all rectilinear
like the building that reflected
his death in every
window while she welcomed the universe
into her hands.

Bettie Page Finds Jesus

When I turned my life over to the Lord Jesus in January 1959, I threw out
all my netstockings, bikinis—some from Frederick's of Hollywood, many
I designed myself: you've certainly seen how my one-piece cheetah print
greeted the Florida coast, then waved it goodbye for good, when I followed
the chapel glow after I left a man in the middle of our two-step to Guy
Lombardo's "Auld Lang Syne." The Lord was never mad. Not even when
my nipple exclaimed its tender joy for Christmas, my black hair so shiny
it was mistaken for tinsel. You'd never know I hated cigarettes by the way
one would hang from my mouth, talisman to badass & red lip. Such divinity
in Max Factor. Can we not talk about my bangs? My forehead never really
disappeared just like I didn't. When people ask me, Bettie, what'd ya think of
wearing that leather horse costume, being spanked on the behind, I chuckle
because one thing I never was was serious. Yeah, maybe it wasn't the best
idea to strap the brunette to a cross made with old broomsticks, but it was
funny, & fun was the fetish I resurrected.

The Many Deaths of Inocencio Rodriguez

San Antonio, TX: Back in the 1930s or 1940s

The car is or isn't stalled.

Little ghosts, children sketched in electricity,
a school bus full of

nudge us

over these tracks—wood
& iron trestles, crosshatched pencil

erased   *a speeding train*

as the stars of their hands fall
down on the glass.

dreadful accident many years ago

The river is pink

& yellow paper umbrellas,
it floods. He holds

me in his arms, tender

with filoplume & filament.

We situate ourselves in the pause:

my planet belly
unnamed, amniotic fluid
great mimic of floodwater,

any car stopped near the railroad tracks will be pushed

a place he'll avoid

until he dies. He still carries

our ghosts glass in a necklace

                          he bought at the mercado,

ghosts in a panic between yellow & pink & green

& all.   *prevent a tragedy and fate like their own*

His feathers could not lift me. The car

                        never moved until it flooded.

True Crime Addict

He tells me to write something about a pig rolling in mud to cool itself off. Instead, I think of Susan Atkins writing *PIG* on the wall with Sharon Tate's blood, after she tore Tate to pieces, ripping a red star from her womb, calling it a mass of grins. They fled far from L.A.'s chromatic buildings of despair, where they told themselves fame went to die. Yes, they were half-right. I picked up the phone Joaquin Phoenix used to call 9-1-1 when River was foaming angelic in dosage. I lay on the lawn where the Black Dahlia was found naked, her homesickness slashed in its crotch. The grass, faking its neon, the word *blades* even too much a symphony. Squeaky Fromme got her nickname because of the way men touched her. There's no truth other than I haven't written since the election. I've been elsewhere, researching serial killers & unsolved murders because at least I don't have to convince people that this is horror.

White Mexican Girl

This world was an accident. If we
picked a place on a map,
this would be *it*
[a globe of pregnancy].
Mexican girls
standing ankle-deep in piles of vanilla
bean carcasses, relieved
of their sweating embryos.
Running barefoot
in the streets to chase the wandering tune
of ice cream [blue ghost, bubble
gum eye]. Where we dug
squirrels' hearts out of their chests
with a rusty grapefruit
spoon & laughed at our violence.
That old, stupid
pain will always be here, but over time, it'll
be harder to diagnose. Oh uterus,
haphazard creator
of our bodies, collapsing stacks of Lisa
Frank erasers [hallucinogenic,
unicorn, & pout]: we faked
our way through Cumbia
[bougie cumbia, poseur cumbia]
King lyrics, repeating *azucar*, as if
our mouths were filled with glass,
as if we were chewing on bullets
aimed at our pasts [*love this old school just visited*
Corpitos, memories from back in the '90s
looking for the person who sang "Nunca
Mi Amor te Olividare," it was half English
half Spanish, Que Viva La Raza].

Jess

She said the ball of light entered her room & saved her life. She held it in
her palm & let it dance. I said, when I was twelve, I captured fireflies in a
jar only for the moment when their lights exhausted. Evelyn Lau said, when
light shattered across the floor, & briefly, there was a thunder between us.
By *us*, she meant me & my brother. When she said, hands stood shaped
like shelters, I wanted it to be my own failures she described. Morrissey
said there is a light that never goes out. John said an incoherent buzz, the
flickering light in his bathroom, stopped him from pulling the trigger. I said,
the light was a jellyfish with teeth, light was the gold piss after the sting.
When the lord said, let there be light, it was hilarity in bright pause.

TRUE CRIME ADDICT

OFFICE OF THE MEDICAL EXAMINER
Wayne County, Michigan
John F. Burton, M.D.
Medical Examiner
400 E. Lafayette Avenue
Detroit, Michigan 48226

FILE NO. _____ 8-71

AUTOPSY NO. _____ A71-9

CERTIFICATE OF DEATH

I, _____ , M.D., CERTIFY THAT

Incencio Rodriguez AKA John Doe #3   AGE 48   SEX Male

WHO LAST RESIDED AT 1739 21st   St.   Detroit, Michigan
                    (NUMBER)   (STREET)   (CITY)   (STATE)

DIED OF THE FOLLOWING CAUSE(S) AND IN THE MANNER INDICATED:

1. DISEASE OR CONDITION DIRECTLY   a. _Gunshot_ _wounds_
   LEADING TO DEATH,   _of the chest_
   DUE TO (ANTECEDENT CAUSES OR   b. _and abdomen_
   MORBID CONDITIONS, IF ANY, GIVING
   RISE TO THE ABOVE CAUSE (a)   _____
   STATING THE UNDERLYING CAUSE   c. _____
   LAST)

2. OTHER SIGNIFICANT CONDITIONS   _____
   (CONDITIONS CONTRIBUTING TO THE _____
   DEATH BUT NOT RELATED TO THE   _____
   DISEASE OR CONDITION CAUSING   _____
   DEATH.)

MANNER OF DEATH: NATURAL ☐   SUICIDE ☐   HOMICIDE ☑   ACCIDENT ☐   UNDETERMINED ☐
   SPECIFY: _____

PLACE OF DEATH: _____ Detroit General Hospital _____ Detroit, Michigan _____
   (HOSPITAL OR INSTITUTION OR STREET ADDRESS OR LOCATION)
ONSET OF ILLNESS OR DISEASE OCCURRED   WHILE AT WORK ☐   NOT WHILE AT WORK ☑

TIME OF INJURY OR ONSET OF ILLNESS: _____ 1/1/71 _____ cc   A.M. P.M.
                                    (MONTH) (DAY) (YEAR) HOUR

TIME OF DEATH: January 1, 1971 at 5:41   A.M. P.M.
              (MONTH)   (DAY)   (YEAR) HOUR
HOW DID INJURY OCCUR OR MODE OF ONSET OF ILLNESS: _____ Shooting
_____
_____
_____

SIGNATURE: _____
TITLE: _____ Wayne County Medical Examiner
DATE: _____

The Girls Gone Up in Smoke

Ashley Freeman, Lauria Bible

What's the alternative for starting with *I remember . . .?* It's *right now, right now.* I worry I write the same thing over & over, trying to solve a riddle about the body, generating nothing but a poor approximation. Darlings, I want to find you in Oklahoma's rubble, but time has outsmarted us again, as I write the shadows & monochrome back into Welch, told *no* over & over again in my own handwriting. Language should be better than this, & I say language because I've given up on us. There's got to be a better way of moving from one idea to another other than *I remember.* Memory is the opposite route homeward—memory, home's autopsy report. The skeletal remains were the moment after the shotgun, the moment before too. Girls nowhere to be found but in memory, so I suppose *I remember* is good for something, for when we stretch absence to its margins. When we try fooling our inner saboteurs by building our faults away from history. Earthquakes in Oklahoma have increased from 41 in 2010 to 888 in 2015, but otherwise, the ground's swollen lips keep silent. I tell the earth, *Kiss them for me.*

The Many Deaths of Inocencio Rodriguez

I was laked by enlightened flies—dead man's float.

Nutshell Diorama

My brother evolves into a windshield shattering, Erté's stars, & the darkness strangles his head
like a turban of black migraine. His teeth gilded into his brain while Jesus Christ cops a feel, then more

darkness except for the ghosts of all our dead dogs, nebulae in their collars' hearts. The universe
needs support, my breasts from their bra straps, stretched out by time & by sheer barroom luck.

Jesus says we are only as strong as fingernails, but he was strung out on heaven. The glowing Jupiters
of my vanity lights: I sit to trace a kohl infinity around my eyes, apply lipstick like I don't want to be

kissed. Wear a cluster of crosses around my neck because I don't want religion, get it? When my brother
went to speak, he didn't know the language & stayed quiet all his life, & when the neighborhood girls

collected dolls, we prized our collection of paper bags, a lifetime's worth of my father's tallboys, his
       crawling-
away-from-the-day-before balanced always in between his knees. Break the aluminum statue, break
       the aluminum

statue. I think Frances Glessner Lee built one of our deaths: his, 18-wheeler, mine, specifics unknown,
but my body would eventually be found in Michigan, where I always knew I would die, hopefully

to the first minute-and-a-half of "To Wish Impossible Things" remastered, bent back into shape
like the hanger I used to string together Styrofoam balls we called the galaxy, Robert Smith's face,

my first drag mother. The most recurring command in the Bible is Fear not, but we were never taught
that—we were taught to fear everything, & I feared my brother the most, especially when he told

the truth we both ran from, the room most covered in blood in Lee's dollhouse, where a knife sticks
out of his gut. It wasn't the 18-wheeler, it was me—red bow weaponry, matching ballet slippers.

I know which one of us died that day, & it wasn't the way either one of us predicted. It was far
worse. I've tried to put the moon back in its place, take it between my fingers, oh luminescence, oh
       lividity,

but it's hard to move a body once the rigor has set in. There are bodies outside of bodies. How many
      have we
tried on to see what fit? The problem was we were too faithful to history & not faithful enough.

Always a newborn, my brother, his cries resisted syllables & wanted instead a warm blanket of yes, yes,
yes, a whistle far from the cemetery where I kicked up the dirt with my combat boots & fishnets

to pay tribute to all the ways we were different: Echo & the Bunnymen, The Cure, David Bowie, Boy
George, Bauhaus, Kim Deal cooing in the background of my favorite Pixies song, my little yes cradle

like Houston's embrace of skyscrapers, rows of smiling platinum & diamond grills. There is no one
body, but I had trouble finding all of his, still do, even when I look inside a model of our childhood home,

pull the miniature VHS from the shelf, undo its ribbon. Written in paint on my bedroom door: *She
      couldn't save him.*

Tabloid for JonBenét Ramsey

We roll our luggage to the place where the street leaves
us & [   ] turns to water, where she dissolves
into the birds of her childhood. [   ] Thieves

of plastic train sets & damsels in distress, we grieve
togetherness just as togetherness sprawls
into the birds of our [   ] childhood, thieves

garroted by spine & wing, as though a paint brush greets
JonBenét's neck rather than a [   ] bruise's crawl.
We roll our luggage   [T]he place where the street

bursts the seams. [   ] Glitter sieved
from its source, her home secure in a globe of nightfall—
[   ] birds of our childhood, [we] thieve

the pineapple paleness of her autopsy, curiosity piecing
violence back together,   always unresolved
& roll[ing   ]. Oh, the place where [we are left   ],

ruining memory's Polaroid when we shake its tender Techni-
color cataract, under our fingers what [   ] evolves,
[little] bird of [our] childhood, [blonde &] thieve[d],
we [   ] our [   ] to the place [where she sleeps].

Tabloid for Jayne Mansfield

ENTERTAINMENT FOR MEN [   ] JUNE 1963 • SIXTY CENTS,
Playboy: The Nudest Jayne Mansfield, a working man's Monroe,
decreased demand for big-breasted blond bombshells [   ],

Miss Magnesium Lamp, Miss Electric Switch, she [   ] bent
wires of the shutter bra & action bra, her golden glow
ENTERTAINMENT FOR MEN [   ] JUNE 1963 • SIXTY CENTS,

[   ] more notorious when she was condemned,
an old chandelier factory. Flourishes & broken curves, intimate Rococo,
decreased demand for big-breasted blond bombshells [   ],

her Buick's top sheared off, her head gone where? Her body, an *amen*
to the Hollywood gods. [   ] Google her torpedoed
[windshield. The] demand for big-breasted blond bombshells [   ],

all wig, all scalp that's left in the mosquito fog. To hyphen
the detritus back into a necklace, stuff her alive again with tobacco,
[Virginia Slim   ] JUNE 1963 • SIXTY CENTS.

Her pool, in the shape of a heart, outlives her tile by tile, pink satin
pillows like bladders [   ] full with urine, spoiled success, more
ENTERTAINMENT FOR MEN [   ] JUNE 1963 • SIXTY CENTS,
[   ] demand for [the female form: presence, absence, presence].

Tabloid for Lupe Vélez

Mexican Spitfire was a compliment more so than *Whoopee Lupe*,
but she insisted she wasn't really wild, even though she rehearsed
nude. [   ] Legend has it she drowned, a plea

to her lover—a swollen bobbing apple to a pair of lucky
lips like a toilet bowl's mouth. [   ] All hail the flirt,
Mexican Spitfire was a compliment more so than [   ] [   ] [ ],

Goddess of Seconal, shocked-shape brow, her territory
was death over loneliness. [   ] Hickey over childbirth.
[Her] nude[, provenance as unknown as a lily's, history's] plea

for another Malinche. *No way*, she said. *That ain't me.*
Staging a precise suicide, her gown ironed of its guayabera texture,
Mexican Spitfire was a [   ] more so than *Whoopee Lupe*,

deconstructed mantilla like a hand of lace over the heart. See?
We aren't so unlike—we've followed a long rod, diviner
[of] nude. [   ] Legend has it she drowned, a plea

[   ] for allegiance, [   ] memory
located at the *X* of two coat hangers, [ ] rather than [ ] unearthed.
Mexican Spitfire was a [   ] more so than *Whoopee Lupe*—
[her] nude[, provenance as unknown as a lily's, American mystery.]

The Last Supper—600 Plates Illustrating Final Meals of U.S. Death Row Inmates

after Julie Green

Like cobalt blue paint icing

second-hand porcelain, an oil

derrick stencils its shadow

on a giant saucer we named *ground*.

Cattle graze lazily, unaware

a freak blizzard will

kill 15,000 dairy cows in all. They say

execution is a peaceful

rendering like taking the accordion

out of zydeco & making it

Stevie Ray Vaughan's

blues. Houston's bodies

refuse to be peeled away

from their walls, despite

months of humidity, but photos

of *Playboy* pin-ups & toddlers

allow their edges to curl,

tongues licking a plate clean.

Human Combustion

It is important for crime scene cleaers to possess the following:

Compassion. All that was left of the old woman was her walker & part of her left leg. As far as I know, there wasn't any family to notify—she had been estranged from them for some time, & I thanked fuck those calls were never part of my job. How do you say to someone, *Your mother exploded. Your mother is ash. Your mother is the cigarette's cherry insulted at the dive bar of her house.*

Stamina. I pulled on my biohazard suit, full facemask, respirator, & two sets of gloves. I got to shoveling the place for three hours until I swept away my own mother from the floorboards. We had to bury her so fast because the bacteria quickly ate away at her memory: pick, adhesive, bloody, dogs, purpose, electrode—all the crumbs left in the dustpan.

Training. Watched Robert Stack growing up. EAR/ONS. Manson. Eileen Wuornos, but I knew why she fucking did it. Bundy. The big names. Gacy. Charles Albright, Rodney Alcala. The Houston Fridge Murders. Tommy Lynn Sells. Angel Maturino Resendiz. Never bought any murderabilia, but John Wayne Gacy's paintings I wouldn't mind owning.

Integrity. When you fail at everything but this.

Commitment. Her collection of porcelain rabbits shone iridescent as I dusted away what was left of myself. She had some recipes in a file folder—the one for menudo I folded like a crane & put in my shirt pocket. My mother always said that sabor was the cure for loneliness. In Spanish, Cinderella is La Cenicienta. That iconic image of Cinderella, the one where está limpiando, is my mother on her hands & knees, scrubbing vomit & Modelo from the carpet.

Attention to detail. Decapitated toes, the foot's soft flesh sawed into like an orange. The birds offer a warning with blood. I was careful with her like gold & silver confetti.

AZO Elegy

America, we should all be groping the wounded curves of your atlas.

The Many Deaths of Inocencio Rodriguez

A huddle of cacti gives the world the finger.

In her jaws, the black dog carries a bird into the house,
                sucking *coo coo coo*
from an Inca dove throat, dumb head buried in her pillow-tongue.

             Upstairs, Isabel is sleeping the scorpion
                                  into the morning's
walls, clustered the color of vomit.
            Sky so clear, it appears
less-than, swollen blue belly,
                   begs to have its water
broken, for a hand to
       find a heartbeat—
                 miscarriage, a construction
of sticks & half-circles, Mexican
       finger painting.

          He comes through the butterfly door, finally—
wasn't quite butterfly
             but its white predecessor, still mourning
a mother,
             that hadn't hung in itself long
enough to perfect its great sadness
           like a testicle.

Interrogation

Jodi Arias sings Dido's "Here With Me" while she waits for the detective. People will be surprised she no longer has blond hair—*that's not the Jodi we knew*—& that she can really, really sing. The vibrato on the word "breathe" is like the satisfaction of pulling a loose thread & undoing a hem. It's believable. I believe it. She scrapes the label off the water bottle like the way he used to undress her.

Court testimony will characterize their relationship as physical without much tenderness, & Nancy, the court reporter, will wince every time she punches "anal" into her stenotype, especially since it's mostly vowel. Jodi will sketch Snow White with a black eye severe. A pentagram. A wad of toilet paper we'll mistake for a corsage.

When Nancy leaves work, she will hum Jodi's hymn, picture his body's confusion in blood. I've seen the crime scene photos, & they didn't shock me as much as I thought they would. Like strangling an ant pile, I can imagine wrapping my hands around a man's neck. Filling his skull with a bullet of ants. Slicing a neck by tying a ribbon of blade into a strict knot. Each digital camera flash, a match ignited into fantasy, & for a moment, I cradle, very close to me, violence.

The Many Deaths of Inocencio Rodriguez

If you put an alcoholic in Technicolor, he is less likely to appear threatening. Like when my Aunt Elma's high school photo came to life as a cartoon, bounded with thick, stark borderlines. Full ligne claire & Ben-Day dots. He was never threatening, always threatening. When he pulled the trigger, a white tongue with *Bang!* exploded from the barrel's mouth. The only machete he ever used was to crack a coconut. The past, constantly being replaced with itself, & we were told never to speak ill of the dead.

Beaten. My grandmother's body thundered against the faux wooden paneling in their little house. He was drunk again, & that's the best excuse he could give. Her body & unborn baby found murdered in a closet. Her skeletal remains found on an island in Panama. Her car backed into an abandoned barn, but her body never found. Her body suffocated, stabbed, or shot, discovered in the wrecked womb of her bed. A television cracked into her skull, the kitchen all vertical colored lines. The rabbit ears found its point of origin, the heart, from which Elma was sprung, along with my mother, two more aunts, uncle. As the VHF signal rotates & transforms, they resurrected. *I'm sorry I lit you on fire.*

Tabloid for Lori Erica Ruff

There is no unmarked woman.

—DEBORAH TANNEN

[   ] & her breast implants refused to burn,
but the serial numbers clung to life, each serif,
a stubborn arm. [   ] Her body sworn

to secrecy: Fife, an Idaho ID card, several pages torn
from an Arizona phone book. 402 months. Dammit,
Lori, [you] refuse to burn,

or are you Becky Sue? More a Jane Doe—we return
you to a burial of blank space [   ]. Half-diamond pick,
a stubborn arm [asking *why, who*   ]: [h]er body sworn

to its strongbox. Miscarriages, her uterus' yearns
for anonymity, [   ] but her daughter persisted.
[   ] & her breast implants refused to burn,

her last suicide note, indecipherable. The cinnamon
stain of her blood, each blot a Rorschach of forget.
[A] stubborn arm, [her gun   ]. Her body sworn.

The Many Deaths of Inocencio Rodriguez

"Yer So Bad" on repeat   comrade

of obsession   all my collectibles: blank & blank   cathedrals

tequila prism   saw me down on 4th St.   no good

Son of a Bitch   cathedral

paste mistaken for   simple syrup   tattoo

mistaken for a tree   Rabbits

plastic & blind   on my mantle   I will die   today

bullet's   heavenly   bait & switch

homesickness   cure   cops

amputated   first   my left arm   then

took the   Detroit   factory of my lower   back

wrecking   yard's   darling

John Doe   #3

even in death   I had a gringo   name

blood's   abrasive hymn   lullaby of wasp   wasp, wasp

Houston

I woke up with another migraine today because I suppose I should be in love. Did you know that the freeways begin with dirt packed on top of itself? Then goes the asphalt, then the concrete, then the little symbol of patriotism. The roaches I leave behind jump into unsuspecting handbags, & naked, I examine my body for places to pick it apart. I float above the roses the Mexican landscapers plant like the woman in the Chagall painting looking for a way out of his dream. *Up*, the only exit. I discipline Texas, just like our forefathers would have wanted, stealing the gallop from a horse while I strangle it with a lasso. How much my dad is a mirror to those men on bulldozers making a city for us, but somehow, he defied gravity by holding spinning police sirens in his hands like drunken planets. *Alarm bells went off*, the white officer says. My grandfather left a couple of his fingers in Normandy, & I have the telegram that officially discharged him framed in gold because I like tragedies still & where I can see them.

The Many Deaths of Inocencio Rodriguez

Walking into the smell of old wounds, something about my grandmother's
bedroom always kept me from there—the perfume
once animal golden now rancid & dark as whiskey. Lace
medallioned, doilies marking time turned to loss
turned back into time, a web for patron saints. If you ask her,
one saved her life: When she was still Mexico's
girl, she was in charge of fire—one night, she let the warmth
rock her to bed, forgot to snuff it out. The Holy Child
with brimmed hat & plume appeared to her, walked barefoot upon
the coals in order to solve an equation
about faith. The house didn't burn down that night.
Fire followed her everywhere.
A mesquite that kept watch over gold coins, on fire.
On fire, prayer in the palm of her hand,
an exhausted, red eye. When Kristen & I would venture to the back
of the house, into Grandma's room, we saw that eye
looking back at us, perfecting our sheepishness,
imprints of guilt all over our bodies like hickeys. We swore we saw him
glaring at us through the blinds, along with the metal roof across
the street, our founder of crisis & consumption. To him, I owe
everything, especially my mother, whose sadness
like the moon's gradient moans I've proudly inherited. We were thieved
by anonymity—I knew him through only one photo,
a monochrome wedding portrait so faint it looked stenciled, so alive
the albumen silver threatened disaster. It always predicted
the future, didn't it? Inocencio & Isabel, he was as young
as a punch—she, in shivers of white fabric pooling around her feet.
He never haunted me as much as that picture did
because it was an insistent threat of fire, the skunk fire
of childbirth, the flammable night cap, little purple flames of bruise.
The lit candle, novena for *come back, come back, come back.*
Womanhood, an education in waiting, as he

chased his bachelor apparition until he discovered death
was even more reckless. I write to you tonight, grandfather, Inocencio,
in hopes that if I say your name enough, it might
be the truth. That your life isn't an old pile of femurs
glued together. That you were luminous despite your wartime.
That the inverse of collapsing is the earth repeating
God through its Richter. I've found you again in the void,
bludgeoned with flowers your memory, larger
& endless like a cloud's exit.

The Many Deaths of Inocencio Rodriguez

Crooked red fingers of stretchmark on her hips, dough Isabel kneads back into hips, magnolias in her hair, blossoming hips, 1930s Mexico, the sun, a hip burst into blood, violet lace pulled across her hips like molasses, molasses leaving white sugar behind, her naked body, more grit than glitter, grotesque like grotesque, the fly left under her soap dish, her hip embrace too wide for a mirror, antique gold frame, roses twisted, wedding ring, a branch that mates with electrical wire, Isabel rinses the campfire out of her hair, replaces it with a tequila baptism, the sizzle of blow flies on a sagging window screen, cheesecloth angry with dough, dough she kneads into a face that stares back at her, magnetic cloud, little thunder of cloth scraping against steel, symmetrical ribs, hip bones steeled, childbeared, pro-savagery, knee steel, we're put back together, unfortunate, the best ghosts we've ever known.

True Crime Addict

Maura Murray, Brianna Maitland, Jaleayah Davis, Rebecca Zahau

She returned the lab coat, & that's a little pre-suicide gesture, we're told, in her arms like a car about to explode into a Vermont snow bank, & we think it's our right to claim something as indifferent as snow, or a girl gone missing. In the time they've all been missing, we're left to rebuild them, a

gesture that works from girl (*my, is she attractive*), worst, her car haphazard barn, a photo's claim to touch. We play detective. their objects, like a to its ribcage; her bra folded, civilized gestures entrails of the car. No died, & we keep referring end up bound-&-gagged figure out why I'm dead. boyfriend did it, & if my I have it. No need for any

only a safe distance. That body assuming the against an abandoned fame. We look but don't Our obsessions missing breast's rightful claim & shirt & coat neatly emulating the unharmed one knows how the girl to her as *The Girl*. If I & hanging, I hope we My bloody car means my body is missing, it's okay, gesture of *I want*, to claim

me for your own. Darkness has its claim on any moving shape resembling a girl, mothers burying tornadoes, tender ghost gestures. We enjoy grief, we like the acts of missing—a prayer to a jar of teeth, a throat yanked from a car. One man actually found her car, gassed it up to see if it actually ran, & now he claims loss is a woman's greatest protection. She's missing ten years now, like so many girls before & after. *Nothing to See Here*, but we know there is, a gesture constantly knotting its center. The car, unlike the girl, is searchable, we claim, her body a paradox, available, through the futile gesture of *her*, missing.

Obituaries

—It takes me so long to read the 'paper,
said to me one day a novelist hot as a firecracker,
because I have to identify myself with everyone in it,
including the corpses, pal'.

—JOHN BERRYMAN, "DREAM SONG 53"

Cell phones sing in the pockets of the dead, the vibrations, startled, carry with them
our last invention, hope. I imagine the glory of all their bodies, God, the question

they answered, how they paint with their blood the insides of everything: *Is this what we mean by power*?
No one knows. Except that we have to put our hands everywhere, on everything,

in a nest on the pretense we're rescuing a bird, in a pocket for the reassurance of a gun's handle,
all our little restitutions & boredom. An absence isn't an absence & neither is *ghost* or *rhetorical*—

like violets for eyes, the natural world demands distortion, we've been told. This year,
there have been too many dead bodies, but we can't say that. We are quiet, while pianos

march on their tiptoes, scaling the minor chords in order to honor a primordial
sadness, like a rucksack of bones. *Have you seen a halo exploded?* Just look into her mouth,

she sucked the gold out of some spray paint cans trying to outrun the sprint of a man's fingers,
her hair & face bright. I ask the world to describe for me such an odor as death, & I arrive at

pencil shavings mixed with ganja & cheap perfume, worse than a refrigerator's burp, worse
than skimming the skin off milk. Julia Kristeva says, "abjection preserves…the immemorial

violence with which a body becomes separated from another body in order to be," & in my
safety, *I am*. My body, something like her car, its complexion pockmarked by bullets,

she is gone, briefly, until she appears in red glitter. I cry along with her father in order
to announce, *I am, I am*, but I'm just as convincing as we are when we summon capable

protagonists: *Do they exist?* They exist as nothingness does, a crowd of lanterns let loose into the air, &
again, hope in lighted form, our suffering bodies deflating like paper bags the closer

we get to earth. I've heard that artists become more vulnerable the closer they get to the inside
of the object, & if that's true, I want to climb inside each backpack lined on this wall,

one for every Mexican child dead in the Arizona desert, in a white dress I want to swing
in an old convent in tandem with another woman. I want unity but haven't been

taught where to find it, & that's just another excuse I use when I get too close.
Like her nude photo floating into another backyard like a leaf, the trail of fetishizing ends

only with a jaw broken by a mouthful of branches, molars chewing the pendent loose
from its stem, her heart from its faithful artery. This is the only time I'll use *heart*,

I'll use *fuck* instead as a way to add more distance between subject & object because where
is the *there*?

A Transitional Time for Planets

The sun begins to arch into its version of a dirty
fingernail. It's about to be suffering,
shadows like last night's mascara in the belly

of this room. On the wall, Chagall's paintings:
a bride being devoured by her blue & black dress
while another woman is a naked & flowering

chrysanthemum. Her hand reaching for his,
unhooking herself from the artist's mirror's mirror.
I want to tell you, you're hard to resist,

life in a wreath of embrace, floating, liquor.
Suddenly, your mattress is a cushion of stars. I thumb
each one as they melt each direction of my fingers

into an electric pool of mauves acrylic & plummed.
We're hungry & not hungry & even more than hungry.
I'm your breakfast on the table, the ripe fruit drum

about to burst into sweet ocean, miscarry
all over this place. Your counterclockwise hand.
My head of stars hungover. Jupiter married

to a socket holding up the wall. I understand
the language of light through the louver blinds:
this universe is haunted.

The Many Deaths of Inocencio Rodriguez

This is the year for unresolved mysteries. We've solved
the black crickets' whine & the cold cut, that sock
in the dryer. I never died,
but had my resurrection moments
like abracadabra. I defaulted to a flock of geese,
avoided bars because if a story goes into a bar, it never
leaves there, does it? It stains the wood bitter.
I was the patron saint of Blue Jean, doing the mindless
factory work of what it means to have pride in Detroit,
denim savior of automobile & explosion,
the living history of *keep your fucking head down*.
At a Tigers game, I sat closest to the mimosa
sunset, the section farthest away that transformed players
into blurs of powdered light. My cap lowered toward
my hangover, the only person who preferred
deciphering the voice of radio announcers through AM
static like when I'd try to remember Isabel's voice
when it rained, home growing smaller
& smaller in my hands as I assembled a fender.
I never knew her favorite color or what to do with love I
never earned. Memory, like spanking the surface
of a hotel pool. A rabbit to stab & stab.

Six Detroiters, one of them a 7-year-old boy, w[...]
in the first nine hours of 1971 after Detroit ended 19[...]
record 580 homicides.

Five persons were shot and one was brutally b[...]
strangled. Two other victims of gunshot wounds, po[...]
were in critical condition and might not live.

ONE WAS KILLED by a stray bullet, one by po[...]
one in an apparent execution slaying and the other ti[...]
New Year's Eve quarrels. Last year, two Detroit[...]
killed on New Year's Eve.

The 1970 homicide total was
62 more than the 488 killings
of 1969, which had been a
record for Detroit.

The first victims of the new
year are:

James Simmons Jr., 7, of
9541 Ward; Innocemio C. Rod-
riquez, 55, of 1627 St. Anne;
Harold Stinnis, 41, of 2227 Le-
land; Michael Brown, 30, of
3501 Tillman; George R.
Webb, 21, of 3730 Helen; and
Mary Frances Smith, 40, of 512
Dickerson.

Police said the Simmons
youth was hit in the face by a
stray bullet at 9 a.m. as he
stood with his parents on the
porch of a friend's house at
13490 Freeland. Police said
they did not know where the
bullet came from.

Rodriguez was shot by Pa-
trolman David Babcock of the
Vernor Precinct at 5 a.m. in
the rear of 1739 Twenty-First,
near the precinct station. Bab-
cock also wounded Manuel
Gonzales, 22, of that address.

When he tried to break up a
gunfight between Rodriquez
and Gonzales, Babcock said.
Rodriquez turned and fired on
him with a carbine, it was
then, Babcock reported, that
he shot and killed Rodriquez.
Gonzales was held for at-
tempted murder, apparently
for his role in the gunfight
with Rodriquez.

Friends found Stinnis' body
at 9 a.m., tied to his bed at
2227 Leland. A pillow case cov-
ered his brutally beaten face,
police said, and an electric
cord was wrapped around his
neck.

Police said Stinnis had a re-
cord of narcotics involvement.
They theorized that he was
killed for revenge.

POLICE FOUND Brown's
body at 9 a.m. in a vacant lot
at 314 Twenty-Third with a
gunshot wound in his lower ab-
domen. Brown reportedly had
been involved in a quarrel and
gunfight at his home.

Webb was shot at 1:23 a.m.
in his chest during a brawl at
a New Year's Eve party at
3729 Monte Vista. Police said
the melee began "because
there was a shortage of girls."
Four others at the party
were wounded, police added.

Miss Smith was shot in the
abdomen shortly after mid-
night at her home. Police
found her body on the dining
room floor. They confiscated
four weapons found in the
house and are seeking her boy-
friend, Cal Freeman, 33, in the
slaying.

Second Trage[...] Kills 4[...]

Special to the Free Pre[...]

LAKE ODESSA [...]
members of a rural [...]
County family, burned [...]
of their home on Ch[...]
mas Eve, died New Y[...]
Day when their car [...]
train near here. Two [...]
including one who wa[...]
in the car, survive.

The victims are C[...]
les Lewis, 39, his v[...]
Ruby, 30, and two s[...]
Leroy, 15, and Erne[...]

Charles Jr., 16, is li[...]
in extremely critical c[...]
dition with internal [...]
juries. David, 12, was [...]
with the family at the t[...]
of the accident.

Police said the Lewi[...]
car slid into a slow-[...]
ving Chesapeake & O[...]
train which had only a [...]
comotive and one car.

The Lewis family h[...]
been staying with re[...]
tives the past week sin[...]
fire gutted their hou[...]
Dec. 24. Friends and neig[...]
bors had collected clot[...]
ing and presents for the[...]
during the holidays.

5 Injured In Pontiac Shooting

Two Pontiac policemen a[...]
three private citizens we[...]
slightly injured early Frid[...]
when they were struck by p[...]
lets from a shotgun blast o[...]
Pontiac's southeast side.

The shooting occured short[...]
after midnight as all five stoo[...]
outside a scout car which ha[...]
rushed to the area to investi[...]
gate an earlier shotgun blast[...]

PATROLMEN Thoma[...]
Crossno and Stephen Fleming[...]
ton each were wounded in the[...]
leg by a pellet. They were[...]
treated at Pontiac General[...]
Hospital and released.

Six Detroiters Slain in First Hours of '71

Victims Incl[...]

7-Year-Ol[...]

Notes

The autopsy report, medical examiner notes, & newspaper article reprinted in this book are from original documents in my grandmother's possession.

As of June 2017, the Yuma County Jane Doe, found murdered in 1999, has been identified as Angel McAllister.

"Last Seen" references missing women from Michigan. The bodies of Jessica Suarez & Chelsea Bruck have since been recovered. While the remains of Jessica Heeringa have not been found, Jeffrey Thomas Willis has been charged with her murder. Shawne Mellios, Paige Renkowski, & Sylvia June Galvan remain missing.

The italicized portion of "Landscape with Boy-on-Boy Action" comes from Cynthia Cruz's poem "The Report on Horses."

Chelsea Bruck went missing in Frenchtown Township, Michigan, in 2014, after a Halloween party. Daniel Clay has since been sentenced to life in prison for her murder.

The *Texas Seven* was a group of prisoners who escaped from the John B. Connally Unit near Kenedy, Texas, on December 13, 2000. While on the run, they shot & killed Irving police officer Aubrey Hawkins. They were all sentenced to death. Donald Keith Newbury's last words are verbatim.

Texas Killing Fields is an area between Houston & Galveston that is a notorious dumping ground. For over four decades, women have gone missing or have been found dead there.

"PHX Elegy" borrows lines from Louise Glück's "The Wild Iris."

"Collective Memory" is based on a *New York Times* article, "When Americans Lynched Mexicans," by William D. Carrigan & Clive Webb. The lines in italics are taken from the poem "Departure/Aperture" in my book, *Karankawa*.

Ashley Freeman & Lauria Bible went missing from Welch, Oklahoma, in 1999, after the Freeman home was found burned to the ground. While searching through the remains, family & friends discovered the bodies of Ashley's parents, Kathy & Danny Freeman. They had been shot. To this day, the girls have never been located.

In the 1940s, Frances Glessner Lee used dollhouses to create twenty models of actual crime scenes for the purposes of studying them down to their tiniest details. Referred to as "Nutshell Studies of Unexplained Death," these recreations pioneered the field of forensic-based detection.
Julie Green's *The Last Supper - Final Meals of U.S. Death Row Inmates* is an installation memorializing inmates' final meals.

Lori Erica Ruff has been identified as Kimberly McClean.

"True Crime Addict" references Rebecca Zahau & Jaleayah Davis who both died under mysterious circumstances. Please visit Jaleayah's Facebook page, *Justice for Jaleayah*, for information on how to get her case reopened. Maura Murray & Brianna Maitland remain missing.

EVERY POEM is always, always for my family. My grandfather, Inocencio Rodriguez, & my grandmother, María Isabel Rodriguez, who has nine lives. To my greatest support system: my father, mother, & brother. To my Aunt Lucy who is such a selfless caretaker. To the Rodriguez cousins who have always traded & shared & retold stories about Grandpa Chencho, keeping him alive. To my Aunt Carmen who directed me throughout this collection both in person & in spirit.

To my heart & soul in three: Nilla, Beans, Migo. To Tina, for entrusting me with the loves of my life.

My warmest gratitude to Oliver de la Paz for selecting this book for the Berkshire Prize; I am so grateful for your time & attention to this manuscript. Kristina Marie Darling, a wonderful & thorough editor who helped me realize the full potential of the collection. To Jeffrey Levine, David Rossitter, Ann Aspell, & all the generous souls at Tupelo for their guidance.

Bill Olsen & Nancy Eimers truly shaped the direction for this book, & for that, I am forever indebted. My sincerest thanks to my cohort at Western Michigan University who had a hand in the revision of many of these poems. Alyssa Jewell is the best reader a writer could ever wish for.

My wonderful community of friends who love unconditionally & without judgment: Allison Parker, Alyssa & Brian Jewell, Lindsey Churchill, Kalyn McAlister, Leslie Similly, Jesse Williams, Jr., Sydney Vance, Michelle Watts, Janine Joseph, Korey Hurni, Liz Milani.

To all the victims of police brutality. Those that are still missing. Victims & survivors of domestic violence. Jane & John Does—I am with you.

Acknowledgments

I am grateful to these journals for including the following poems in their publications:

The Acentos Review: "White Mexican Girl"

Banango Street: "Tequila, Cinnamon, Orange" & "True Crime Addict"

The Boiler: "Marfa Lights" & "Houston"

Bennington Review: "Tabloid for the Black Dahlia" & "Tabloid for JonBenét Ramsey"

The Broken Plate: "Obituaries"

Grist: "Tabloid for Judy Garland"

Juked: "Texas Seven"

Latin American Literature Today: "The Many Deaths of Inocencio Rodriguez," "Milieu," & "The Many Deaths of Inocencio Rodriguez"

Midwestern Gothic: "Last Seen"

Miracle Monocle: "The Many Deaths of Inocencio Rodriguez"

New Plains Review: "The Many Deaths of Inocencio Rodriguez"

New South: "The Many Deaths of Inocencio Rodriguez" & "The Many Deaths of Inocencio Rodriguez"

Nightjar: "Elegy to the 1950s Waist"

Petrichor: "Tabloid for Inocencio Rodriguez"

Pittsburgh Poetry Review: "Landscape with Graceland Crumbling in My Hands," "A Transitional Time for Planets," & "Ken Caminiti Dies in a Houston Hotel"

Puerto del Sol: "Tabloid for Jayne Mansfield," "Tabloid for Lupe Vélez," & "Tabloid for Lori Erica Ruff"

RHINO: "Hoax"

Scalawag: "The Many Deaths of Inocencio Rodriguez"

Somos En Escrito: "White Mexican Girl," "Still Life," & "The Many Deaths of Inocencio Rodriguez" (formerly "My Grandmother as Erté's *Starstruck*")

Tinderbox Poetry Journal: "Bird Atlas," "Jess," & "Interrogation"

Virginia Quarterly Review: "The Many Deaths of Inocencio Rodriguez," "The Many Deaths of Inocencio Rodriguez," "The Many Deaths of Inocencio Rodriguez," "Collective Memory," & "Texas Killing Fields"

Waxwing: "Love Letter to Scott Peterson," "Bettie Page Finds Jesus," & "The Girls Gone Up in Smoke"

RECENT AND SELECTED TITLES FROM TUPELO PRESS

Lost, Hurt, or in Transit Beautiful (poems) by Rohan Chhetri

Glyph: Graphic Poetry=Trans. Sensory (graphic poems) by Naoko Fujimoto

Bed (poems) by Elizabeth Metzger

Ashore (poems) by Laurel Nakanishi

The Pact (poems) by Jennifer Militello

Music for Exile (poems) by Nehassaiu deGannes

Nemerov's Door (essays) by Robert Wrigley

Shahr-e-jaanaan: The City of The Beloved (poems)
    by Adeeba Shahid Talukder

I Will Not Name It Except To Say (poems) by Lee Sharkey

The Earliest Witnesses (poems) by G.C. Waldrep

Master Suffering (poems) by CM Burroughs

And So Wax Was Made & Also Honey (poems) by Amy Beeder

The Nail in the Tree: Essays on Art, Violence, and Childhood
    (essays/visual studies) by Carol Ann Davis

Exclusions (poems) by Noah Falck

Arrows (poems) by Dan Beachy-Quick

Salat (poems) by Dujie Tahat

Lucky Fish (poems) by Aimee Nezhukumatathil

boysgirls (hybrid fiction) by Katie Farris

America that island off the coast of France (poems)
    by Jesse Lee Kercheval

Hazel (fiction) by David Huddle

What Could Be Saved: Bookmatched Novellas & Stories
    (fiction) by Gregory Spatz

Native Voices: Indigenous American Poetry, Craft and Conversation
    (poetry and essays) CMarie Fuhrman, Dean Rader, editors

Dancing in Odessa (poems) by Ilya Kaminsky

Xeixa: Fourteen Catalan Poets (poems) edited by Marlon L. Fick and
    Francisca Esteve

Flight (poems) by Chaun Ballard

Republic of Mercy (poems) by Sharon Wang

See our complete list at tupelopress.org